CW00538381

In 1873, the Town Commissioners – predecessor of today's Borough Council – opened this burial ground to serve all denominations. Laid out by the Town Surveyor, William Brentnall, himself buried here, it has been described as one of the most beautiful cemeteries in England. Still a working cemetery, it now contains over 44,000 burials. The crematorium was added in 1959.

Description in Pelton's Guide published in 1875:

The Public Cemetery

Twenty acres of land on Frant Forest were purchased from Lord Abergavenny by the Commissioners in their capacity of Local Burial Board. The land, which occupies a lofty position, and commands an extensive prospect in every direction, has been enclosed. It has been, according to custom, divided into consecrated and unconsecrated sections, and two very pretty chapels have been erected, and a neat entrance lodge. The Cemetery has been laid out with suitable shrubs and plants, and when these have grown, the ground will present a very pleasing appearance.

Contents

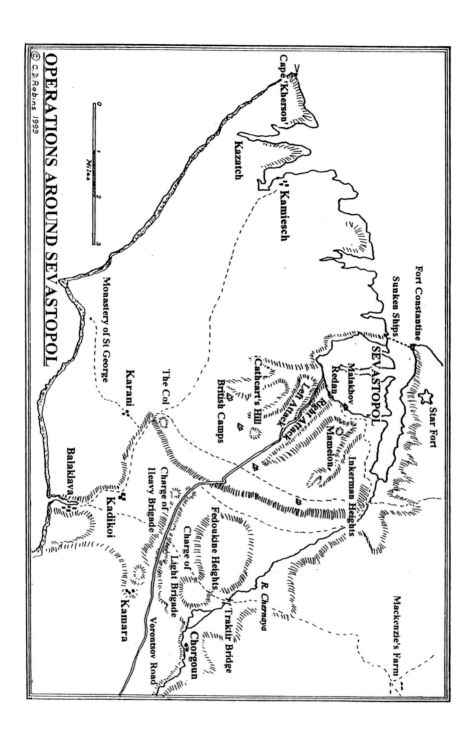

OPERATIONS AROUND SEVASTOPOL

© C.D.Robins 1999

Miles
0 1 2 3

Cape 'Kherson'

Kazatch

'Kamiesch'

Monastery of St George

Karani

The Col

British Camps

Cathcart's Hill

Left Attack

RIGHT ATTACK

Mamelon

Malakhov

Redan

SEVASTOPOL

Inkerman Heights

Sunken Ships

Fort Constantine

Star Fort

Balaklava

Kadikoi

Kamara

Charge of
Heavy Brigade

Charge of
Light Brigade

Fedoukine Heights

Chorgoun

Vorontsov Road

Traktir Bridge

R. Chernaya

Mackenzie's Farm

1.   Introduction

The Tunbridge Wells Cemetery at Hawkenbury celebrated its 150th Anniversary in 2023[1] while in 2018 and 2019 the Friends of the Cemetery published two monographs commemorating the service of men and women of the First and Second World Wars 'who rest' in the cemetery.[2, 3] This monograph focuses on an earlier conflict that took

place during 1854–1856 between Russia and the Ottoman Empire, Britain, France, and Piedmont-Sardinia; and what is now usually referred to in common parlance as the Crimean War. This term is misleading however as hostilities took place on four fronts, namely the White Sea, the Baltic, the Russian Pacific coast, and the Crimean region (the latter campaign involving present day Romania and Bulgaria, eastern Turkey, and the Caucasus). A more appropriate name is the War with Russia, a term that was often used in contemporary accounts. The British and French governments declared war on 28 March 1854; the Crimea was invaded on 14 September 1854; and the battles of the Alma, Balaklava and Inkerman were fought on 18 September, 25 October, and 5 November 1854. There were two major assaults on Sevastopol on the 18 June and 8 September 1855, after which the allies occupied the south of the city. The Peace Treaty was signed on 30 March 1856 with the evacuation of the British troops from the Crimea being completed on 12 July 1856 with those stationed in Turkey leaving a few weeks later.[4]

Unlike the Medway towns and the south coast ports of Southampton and Portsmouth, Tunbridge Wells was not directly affected by the war although local residents contributed to charities that supported the troops at the front and widows and orphans at home[5] while an impressive Peace Parade was held on 4 June 1856.[6]

The town had developed during the 19th century and became a popular place to live for both veterans and members of their families; and a number of these individuals were laid to rest in the town's cemeteries. The Borough cemetery in Benhall Mill Road, Hawkenbury was opened in 1873 and superseded the 'arcadian' burial ground of Holy Trinity Church in Woodbury Park Road as the principal cemetery in Tunbridge Wells.

The publication of this monograph serves to commemorate the 170th anniversary of the start of the Crimean War in 1854 and is based in part on an article published by the author in the *Genealogists' Magazine*;[7] and is concerned principally with individuals interred at Hawkenbury. For several of these the funeral service was at either Holy Trinity or St Paul's, Rusthall with the committal at Hawkenbury. Before the opening of Hawkenbury, churchyards or Woodbury Park cemetery would have been used for burials. Some individuals associated with the war in this category are included in Appendices 1–3 while two others who lived in Southborough and were buried there are in Appendix 4.

The names of individuals mentioned who participated in the Crimean War in one capacity or another, or their relatives, together with locations in Tunbridge Wells are in bold Roman type. The rank of military personnel is the one they held when they either died or were killed during the campaign or when they left the Crimea; the final rank is also given for those who continued with their career in the forces.

The front cover
The medals were awarded to Captain, later Major, **George Frederick Dallas**, 46th (South Devonshire) Regiment, and comprise the Crimea medal with the clasps for Alma, Balaklava, Inkermann (now Inkerman), and Sebastopol (now Sevastopol), the Second China War medal, Legion of Honour 5th class, the Order of Medjidie 5th class and the Turkish Crimea medal.[8] In 1841 Dallas was a pupil at the

preparatory school of Thomas Robert Allfree (1796–1868) in Romanoff House, now **Vale Towers, 58 London Road** (See Appendix 3). Dallas's parents lived for a while in Tunbridge Wells. His father, Robert William Dallas, a veteran of the Walcheren expedition and the Peninsular War, died on 11 September 1849 at **1 Dorset Place, Church Road**, since demolished and replaced first by Telegraph House and then Norfolk Heights. He was buried in the nearby churchyard of Holy Trinity (See Appendix 1). [Front cover picture courtesy of Mike Hargreave Mawson, a descendent of the recipient].

Back cover
One of the treasures in the Tunbridge Wells Museum is the magnificent 'so-called' Crimean War patchwork quilt which may have been made by an unknown convalescent soldier from about 10,000 pieces of uniform cloth manufactured from worsted wool. It was presented to the Tunbridge Wells Borough Council on 4 December 1918 and in 1930 it was reported by the Watch Committee that 'a rug made from tunics used in the Crimean War had been offered to the Museum Committee and they agreed to store it until it could be displayed'[9] although this has never come to pass presumably owing to its large size being approx. 245cm/8ft square. It has been conserved by Zenzie Tinker Conservation Ltd, Brighton and it was displayed at Tate Britain ('British Folk Art' during June–August 2014) and the Tunbridge Wells Museum and Art Gallery ('Material Obsessions: British Folk Art' during January–May 2015).[10] [Cover picture courtesy of the Amelia Scott, Tunbridge Wells].

Federick Charles Aylmer (1814–82) and his wife
Grave: B15/70 consecrated

Lieutenant Colonel **Frederick Charles Aylmer**, the son of Admiral John Aylmer, was present at the siege of Sevastopol with the 89th Regiment and his diary and journals for 1842–1855 are preserved in the National Army Museum. He lived sometime in **Pendower, 36**

Lansdowne Road, since replaced by a terrace of four town houses, and where he died on 20 March 1882 without issue. His personal estate was £19,581. His elder brother, Lieutenant Colonel, later Honorary Major General, **Henry Aylmer** (1813–1904), Royal Artillery, was also in the Crimea and sometime commanded the batteries attached to the 2nd Division. The brothers married sisters, the daughters of John Gwatkin (1786–1869) of Park Behan, Cornwall, respectively: Maria Anne and Charlotte Louise. Maria Anne died on 25 January 1884 and her executors were her sisters Charlotte Louise and Fanny Theophilia, the wife of George Hadow. Effects £37,222. [36 Lansdowne Road. Photograph by the author].

Henry Baring (1831–1929) and family members
Graves: A9/105–6 & A9/164 consecrated

Lieutenant **Henry Baring**, 17th Lancers, was the second son of Henry Bingham Baring (1803–69) and Lady Augusta, née Brudenell (d.1853), a daughter of the 6th Earl of Cardigan. He arrived in the Crimea in July 1855; too late to have taken part in the charge of the Light Cavalry Brigade commanded by his uncle, Major General **John Thomas Brudenell** (1797–1868), 7th Earl of Cardigan. Henry's brothers, Captain, later Honorary Lieutenant General, **Charles Baring** and Major, later Lieutenant Colonel, **Francis Baring** (1833–95) also participated in the campaign with the Coldstream Guards and the Scots Fusilier Guards respectively, with Charles having an arm amputated during the battle of the Alma. Their aunt, Lady Anne Brudenell, a sister of Lord Cardigan, married Lieutenant General, later Field

Marshal, **Charles George Bingham** (1800–88), 3rd Earl of Lucan, who commanded the Cavalry Division in the Crimea, and whose son, and the Baring brothers' cousin, Major Lord **George Bingham** (1830–1914), Coldstream Guards, was sometime one of his father's ADCs.[11]

After the war Henry had an affair with Emily Clara, née Turner, the wife of Henry William Compton, a shorthand writer. She was a professional ballet dancer, using the stage name of Miss Wyndham. The Comptons divorced in June 1861. Henry was named as co-respondent and the proceedings were reported *in extenso* in *The Times*. Emily and Henry married on 22 February 1862 and after living in Oldbury-on-the-Hill in 1871 and Wimbledon in 1881, they moved to Tunbridge Wells and lived **1 Queen's Road** where Emily Clara, who had had no children, died in 1887 and was buried at Hawkenbury (Grave A9/164 consecrated). Henry married Harriett Emily, a daughter of Edward George Cubitt of Honing Hall, Norfolk, on 22 March 1888. In 1891 they were living with their two young children at **2 Mount Ephraim**. Their son, Charles Brudenell died on 21 December 1891 aged 10 months and was buried at Hawkenbury (Grave:A9/106 consecrated). The Barings and their three children had moved to **5 Clanricarde Gardens** by 1901, while the 1911 census finds them at **5 Somerville Gardens, Boyne Par**k. Henry was still living there when he died on 13 April 1929, aged 97. Baring was noted for devoting his 'untiring energies' to evangelical work, and following a funeral service at Holy Trinity, where he was a regular worshipper, he was interred at Hawkenbury.[12] Probate was granted to his widow; effects £5,565. His tombstone also records the death of his son, Captain Henry Baring of the Royal West Kent Regiment, the RAF, and the Public School for Boys in Shanghai, where he died on 14th September 1930. Augusta, the Barings' daughter and widow of the Revd Dr Walter R. Scott, Royal Navy, died at the **Lonsdale Nursing Home, 7 Lonsdale Gardens** on 4 May 1941. She was buried in the same grave as her elder infant brother, Charles Brudenell, whereas her mother, who died on 12 August 1950, aged 87, was interred in the same grave as Henry. [Henry Baring. Credit: *Sevenoaks Chronicle*, 19 April 1929].

Frederick Cleeve (1821–1905) and his wife
Grave: A11/36 consecrated

Frederick Cleeve, Royal Navy, JP, was a paymaster with Admiral Sir **Edmund Lyons**, GCB, GCMG, KCH, 1st Baron Lyons, who sometime commanded the fleet in the Black Sea, and whose funeral he attended in 1859. Cleeve was awarded the KCB and knighthood in 1902. Sir Frederick lived at **Rokeby, 6 Chilston Road** from at least 1892; and where he died on 28 September 1905.[13] His wife, Dame Ellen Martha (b.1831), died aged 92 on 14 November 1922 and was buried in the same grave as her husband. Their effects were valued at £23,224 and £7,392, respectively. [Left. Burial grant purchased by Sir Frederick Cleeve, KCB. Credit: Tunbridge Wells Borough Archives and Right. Sir Edmund Lyons, 1855 by **Edward Armitage**. Credit: *Illustrated London News*, 30 June 1855].

Frederick Lockwood Edridge (1830–1913)
Grave: B2/240 consecrated

Lieutenant, later Lieutenant Colonel (1881), **Frederick Lockwood Edridge**, 20th (East Devonshire) Regiment, was first commissioned in 1855 and was present at the siege of Sevastopol and the Indian Mutiny, where 'he distinguished himself.' He retired in 1889; was awarded the CB in 1907; and was living at **2 Clanricade Gardens** in 1911 with his younger unmarried sister Ellen Mary, 79; an unmarried daughter from his first marriage, Mary Isabel, 34; his second wife of six years, Rose, née Morley (d.1935), 31; and two daughters aged three and one; together with six servants. He died on 12 February 1913. Effects £14,852.[14] [Lieutenant Colonel Edridge's tombstone. Photograph by the author].

John James Heywood, (1832–1912) and his wife
Grave: B1/63

Lieutenant, later Major General, **John James Heywood**, 1st (Royal) Regiment, was first commissioned in 1854; present at the siege of Sevastopol from 1 June 1855 and took part in the Ashanti War. He and his wife Anna, née Apthorp, were living at **43 London Road** in 1891 – since demolished and now a hotel – and at **Pinewood, Frant Road** in 1901, where he died on 10 January 1912.[15] Mrs Heywood died in 1916. Incidentally, Heywood's father-in-law, Major General East Apthorp (1805–75), CB, KSI was living with his wife Mary Ann, née Moorhead, two children, and two servants at **1 Church Road, St John's** in 1871. Mrs Apthorp (b.1814) died during the following September in Southsea while Apthorp died on 3 March 1875 while living at **Amhurst Lodge, 8 Amhurst Road, St John's**.

He was buried at Hawkenbury (Grave: A14/147 consecrated). His executors were his son, the Revd East Apthorp of Abinger, Surrey, and his son-in-law **John James Heywood**, then a major.

Trevenen James Holland (1834–1910) and his wife
Grave: A11/247–8 consecrated

Lieutenant, later Lieutenant Colonel, **Trevenen James Holland**, CB, DL, JP, was born in India. He had a distinguished military career in the Indian Army and took part in the Indian Mutiny, and Persian and Abyssinian campaigns. An obituary in *The Times*, 22 February 1910, recorded that he was with the 10th Hussars in the Crimea although no record has been found that he was officially part of the British Army; for example, his name does not appear in either the regimental muster or medal rolls or General Orders that were issued daily. However, a photograph of Holland in military uniform offered for sale by Bates and Hindmarsh, Cheltenham, shows him wearing the Turkish Crimea medal, Order of the Medjidie, Legion of Honour, and the Sardinian Al Valore Militaire although no documentary evidence to confirm that he was entitled to any of these medals has yet been found.[16] He was first commissioned in 1851 and retired from the army in 1871 and became prominent in local affairs, being sometime a Kent County councillor and a Deputy Lieutenant. He lived in **Mount Ephraim House**, now a care home, where he died on 21 February 1910. His wife, Margaret Emma née Nicholson (b.*c*.1840), who continued to live there, died on 7 December 1922 and was buried in the same grave as her husband. Holland left £138,466, with a bequest of £500 to the Eye and Ear Hospital, Tunbridge Wells.[17] [Left: Lieutenant Colonel Trevenen James Holland and Right: Mount Ephraim House. Courtesy of Philip Whitbourn].

Lewis Charles Augustus Meyer (1809–90) and his wife
Grave: A10/2 consecrated

Lieutenant Colonel **Lewis Charles Augustus Meyer** was the riding master at the Maidstone Cavalry Depôt and would have known Captain **Louis Edward Nolan** (1818–54), who carried Lord Raglan's fateful order that resulted in the charge of the Light Cavalry Brigade during the battle of Balaklava on 25 October 1854. Nolan had been stationed at Maidstone before the war where there is now a commemorative statue in Church Street. The two men had very different approaches to the instruction of equitation although Nolan's contribution to this controversial topic was curtailed by his death on the battlefield on 25 October 1854. Meyer

retired in 1856 and married Julia Mary Woodford (1839–1913) in 1879. They lived in her residence, **Chesterfield House, Camden Hill**. He was inter alia a member of the Army Scripture Readers' Society and died at St Leonards-on-Sea on 4 September 1890. His personal estate was £28,258.[18] Mrs Meyer died on 31 May 1913 and was buried in the same grave as her husband. [Lieutenant Colonel Meyer's tombstone. Photograph by the author].

John Rashleigh Rodd (1816–92) and his wife
Grave: A10/226–7 consecrated

Commander, later Admiral, **John Rashleigh Rodd**, the fifth son of the Revd Dr Edward Rodd, was second in command of HMS *Impregnable*, the port admiral's flagship, in Devonport during the Crimean war. He then commanded HMS *Belleisle* when stationed in the East Indies and China; the vessel had been employed as a naval hospital ship during the war. He married his cousin Wilhelmina Rodd in 1852.

They were living at **Warberry, Speldhurst** in 1891 and he succumbed to the 'prevailing epidemic' on 15 January 1892,[19] while his wife died on 25 July 1903. His effects were £5,462. [The hospital ship HMS *Belleisle* in the Baltic. Credit: *Illustrated London News*, 18 August 1855].

3. Soldiers and Sailors

Thomas Allen (*c.*1829–1910) and his wife
Grave: C5/344 consecrated

Private **Thomas Allen** (c.1829–1910), 17th Lancers, was born in Maidstone and was a groom before he enlisted. He served in the Crimea but he did not participate in the charge of the Light Cavalry Brigade although he was entitled to the Crimea medal with the clasps for the battles of the Alma, Balaklava and Inkerman, and the siege of Sevastopol.[20] His wife Martha died and was buried at Hawkenbury on 30 September 1892 and he on 20 October 1910.

John Boxall (*c.*1832–1914)
Grave: C13/474 consecrated

Private **John Boxall**, 4th Light Dragoons, was born in Midhurst and was severely wounded during the charge of the Light Cavalry Brigade and taken prisoner. He remained incapacitated for the rest of his life and received £235 6s from the T.H. Roberts Balaclava Light Brigade Charge Survivors' Relief Fund between July 1897 and December 1911.[21] He lived in **63 Rochdale Road**, where he died. The funeral service was at St Barnabas, Camden Road[22] although his grave has yet to be located. In his book on the town's history Frank Chapman referred to a John Box – presumably Boxall – and of whom it was said: 'always kept his Balaclava tunic, stained with blood from his many wounds and pierced all over by Russian lances'; and 'who augmented his pension of ten pence a day by working in the Black

Horse pub' which is located at the junction of Camden Road and Commercial Road. [Left: J. Boxall. Credit: *Kent and Sussex Courier*, 21 August 1914 and Right: Black Horse Inn, Tunbridge Wells. Photograph by the author].

Sidney French (*c.*1825–1904)
Grave: C13/753 & 755 consecrated

Private **Sidney French** served with 20th (East Devonshire) Regiment. The eldest of five brothers who were all in the army, with two dying in India; present at the battles of Alma, Balaklava, Inkerman, and siege of Sevastopol. A member of the Foresters he had been resident in Tunbridge Wells for about forty years and was an out of work butler in 1871, while in 1901 he was living at **18 Calverley Street** with his wife Ann; they were aged 76 and 72 respectively.[23] [Other ranks Shako badge, 20th Regiment. Credit: © W. Hutchinson, M. Vice, and B.J. Small].

Hippisley Cunliffe Marsh (1837–1917) and his wife
Grave: A10/43 consecrated

Hippisley Cunliffe Marsh joined the merchant navy aged fourteen and his service took him to the Crimea. He then served in India with the 18th Bengal Cavalry and retired a lieutenant colonel;[24] married Emma Brett Hebbert (1854–1933) at Trinity Church in 1877; lived in the town since at least 1886; and died a 'highly respected resident of the town' at **Clarence Hill, Clarence Road** on 17 December 1917; his effects were £6,973.[25] He and his wife were buried in the same grave. Also commemorated are two sons: Hippisley Leith Marsh who died in India on 4 April 1881 aged 12 months and 2nd Lieutenant Ellis Ernest Marsh, 3rd Lancashire Fusiliers, who died in Malta on 28 July 1901, aged nineteen. Mrs Marsh's parents were buried nearby in Grave A10/11. [H.C. Marsh. Credit: *Kent and Sussex Courier*, 21 December 1917].

Stephen Spratt (*c.*1836–1915)
Grave: C13/834 consecrated

Corporal, later Police Sergeant, **Stephen Spratt**,
97th (Earl of Ulster's) Regiment. He lived at **47
William Street**; took part in the siege of
Sevastopol; and the Indian Mutiny, being present at
the relief of Lucknow. The son of a Police
Inspector, he joined the Tunbridge Wells Borough
Police Force following retirement from the army.
He was discharged as a sergeant in 1891 on
medical grounds after being injured while on duty.
The Watch Committee Minutes in the Tunbridge
Wells Borough Archives recorded on 31 December 1891 that he was
awarded the maximum pension allowed by the Police Act 1890. He
died aged 79 on 4 January 1915 at **47 William Street** and his funeral
was attended by representatives of the police force and two
members of his old regiment which by this time was amalgamated
with the Royal West Kent Regiment.[26] His wife Elizabeth Ann née
Keys died in 1918, aged 79. [S. Spratt. Credit: *Kent and Sussex Courier*,
15 September 1915].

James Martin (*c.*1836–1919)
Grave: C12/345 consecrated

James Martin, a Crimean War veteran, lived in **Bayham Road** and
died aged eighty three. Sir Robert Gower, OBE, the mayor, made
arrangements for a military funeral at Hawkenbury. An officer, band,
firing party and buglers from the Royal West Kent Regiment were
present at the graveside.[27]

John George Love (*c*.1843–1929) and his wife
Grave: B3/5 consecrated

Love was born in Lamberhurst but spent most of his life living in Tunbridge Wells, apart from his service in as yet undetermined military capacity at Malta during the Crimean War. In 1855 he wrote a letter to Mr Chapman the headmaster of the Chapel of Ease School where he had been a pupil, and was still serving when peace was proclaimed.[28] He was twice married; first to Rosina Shingleton (1840–77) in 1863 and second to Elizabeth Breden (1851–1931) in 1878 at **Holy Trinity, Church Road**; and both marriages resulted in several children.

George was the landlord of the **Alma Beer House, 7 Varney Street, off Calverley Road** in 1871[29] while in the following censuses he was variously a bricklayer, painter, plumber, and builder when he was living in **8 Warwick Road, off the High Street** and then nearby at **20 Little Mount Sion**. He was a crack shot and won many prizes, and had the distinction of eventually becoming both the oldest and most aged druid of the Order of Druids. He was living at **28 Park Street, off Prospect Road** when he and his wife celebrated their golden wedding anniversary in 1927. He died on 11 January 1929 and following a funeral service at St Peter's, Bayhall Road the committal was at Hawkenbury.[30] Mrs Love died on 6 July 1931 at **28 Park Street**, and was buried at Hawkenbury.[31] Her executrix was Allison Jessie Mitchell, a widow. Effects £168. [G.J. Love. Credit: *Kent and Sussex Courier*, 18 January 1829; and Alma Tavern, 7 Varney Street, *c*.1954. Credit: Creative Commons Licence, Dover Kent Archives].

4.   Army Medical Department

Daniel Paterson Barry (1825–1901) and his wife
Grave: B13/278 consecrated

Surgeon **Daniel Paterson Barry**, MRCS, 13th (1st Somersetshire)
Regiment. The son of Samuel Barry and Annabella Harriett, née
Paterson; first appointed in 1846; was present at the siege of
Sevastopol and the Indian Mutiny. He died in Tunbridge Wells on 3
March 1901; his address in the Kelly's Directories for 1900 and 1901
was **Kilcarn, 20 Court Road**. His widow, Amy Georgiana Anne (Annie)
née Lanigan (1830–1920) and three daughters were living at 25
Albion Place, Ramsgate, and Hill Rise, Ullswater Road, Radipole in
1901 and 1911, respectively. She died in an apartment house at **1
Holden Road, Southborough** on 16 November 1920 and was buried in
the same grave as her husband. Probate was granted to her
unmarried daughters Ada Paterson Barry, Dora Paterson Barry, and
Ruth Paterson Barry. Their effects were £9,495 and £155 respectively.

Thomas Moorhead (1822–1877)
Grave: C5/93 consecrated

Surgeon, later Deputy Surgeon General, **Thomas Moorhead**, LRCS,
MD; first appointed 1845; was a Staff Surgeon at Scutari – where he
arrived on *Vectis* on 4 November 1854 with Florence Nightingale

and her nurses – and then with 7th (Royal Fusiliers) Regiment in the Crimea. He married Angelina Mary Sophia Stopford in Bombay in 1867; was living at 16 Queen's Road, Clifton, Bristol in 1871; retired on half-pay in 1876; and died in Tunbridge Wells on 26 May 1877.[32] The inscription on his tombstone was approved by the Burial Board Committee on 28 October 1878. Moorhead's brother, Edward Moorhead, MD, was one his executors and had been stationed in India during the war as a surgeon with the 29th (Worcestershire) Regiment. His effects were <£5,000. [Military Hospital, Scutari by Francis Bedford, 25 May 1862. Credit: Royal Collection Trust ©HM King Charles III 2024: RCIN 2861695].

George Saunders (1823–1913)
Grave: A4/41 general

Surgeon, later Honorary Deputy Inspector of Hospitals, **George Saunders**, CB (1865), MD, 47th (Lancashire) Regiment. Born in Cork, the third son of Lieutenant Colonel Richard Saunders (d.1878); married Isabella Marina (d.1903), daughter of Thomas Bailey in Buttevant, Cork in 1852 and they had two sons and two daughters; was present at the battles of the Alma and Inkerman and the siege of Sevastopol and later campaigns. Living at **14 Church Road** with his wife and unmarried daughter Selina Elizabeth in 1891, they were lodging at **The Pavilion, 85 Mount Ephraim** in 1901 and 1903 when his wife died; in Eastbourne with his daughter in 1911; and was at Mrs Finch's lodging house **Holmrook, London Road** when he died, on 6 March 1913.[33] Notices in the press intimated that carriages would meet the 10.30 train from Victoria Station on the day of the funeral.[34] Probate was granted to the Public Trustee; effects £29,155.

A committed Christian, he was sometime President of the Medical Missionary Association; his letters to his wife were published shortly after the war.[35] Incidentally, the probate register gave his address as late of 53 Southside, Clapham Common. While his son Thomas Bailey Saunders who died in Eastbourne in 1928 was buried in the adjacent grave A4/40, the plot was purchased by his widow and former house keeper, Ida, née Johnson, whom he married in 1925. [Photograph credit: Kent and Sussex Courier, 14 March 1913].

5.   Relatives of those who served in the war

Clara Jane Baldwin (c.1815–91)
Grave: B10/18 consecrated

Clara Jane Baldwin was the last surviving daughter of William Baldwin of Stede Hill, Kent. She was the younger half-sister of Lecilina (1792–1845) who was the first wife of Brigadier **William Burton Tylden** (1794–54), Royal Engineers, and mother of their younger son Lieutenant Colonel **Richard Tylden** (1819–55), Royal Engineers. Tylden senior died of cholera shortly after the battle of the Alma while Tylden junior, who had been seriously wounded during the siege of Sevastopol, died while en route to England. Their bodies were repatriated to England and interred in the family vault in the graveyard of St Mary and the Holy Cross, Milstead, Kent; and they are commemorated on an impressive mural monument in the church. Incidentally, in the 1871 census Miss Baldwin was visiting William, the rector at Stanford, Kent and the eldest son of **William Burton Tylden**.[36] She died at **42 Grove Hill Road** on 15 June 1891. Probate was granted to her brother Wriothesley; her personal estate was £399. [Left. Brigadier Tylden, RE. Credit: *Illustrated London News*, 14 December 1854, and Right. Lieutenant Colonel R. Tylden, RE, by Roger Fenton. Credit: Royal Collection Trust/© King Charles III, 2024: RCIN 2500225].

Charlotte Agnes Cureton (c.1797–1876)
Grave A14/144 consecrated

Charlotte Agnes Cureton, née Tomkins, was the widow of Brigadier Charles Robert Cureton (1789–1848), 16th Queen's Lancers and sometime an ADC to the Queen, who was killed in action at Ramnaucour (now Ramnagar) in the Punjab on 22 November 1848. She was the mother of Lieutenant Augustus John Cureton (1831–49), 14th Light Dragoons, who was killed at the battle of Chillianwalla in Punjab and Captain, later Hon. Lieutenant General, **Edward Burgoyne Cureton** (1822–1894), 12th Lancers, who had seen active service in India and South Africa and was present at the siege of Sevastopol from July 1855. Mrs Cureton was in receipt of a civil list pension of £200 in consideration of her husband's distinguished service.[37] She died on 11 January 1876 at Tunbridge Wells but had a grace and favour residence at Hampton Court. Her executors were her sons Edward Burgoyne Cureton and Major General Charles Cureton. Effects <£5,000.

Wilhelmina (d.1889) and Mary Elizabeth (d.1895) Hore-Ruthven
Grave B13/81 consecrated

Mary Elizabeth Thornton Ruthven (1784–1864), Baroness Ruthven, married Walter Hore (d.1878) in 1806 and three of their daughters had a connection with Tunbridge Wells, and one of  their sons and a grandson were present in the Crimea. Wilhelmina Hore-Ruthven died in the town on 14 October 1889 and probate was granted to her widowed sister Jane Stewart O'Grady, née Hore-Ruthven (c.1824–1917) who was living at **5 Calverley Terrace**. Their other sister, Mary Elizabeth Hore Ruthven, of **12 Calverley Park Crescent**, died on 28 March 1895 and was buried with her sister. Their brother

Lieutenant **Cavendish Bradstreet Hore-Ruthven,** (c.1822–1854) Royal Navy, of HMS *London*, died of wounds received in the trenches on 22 October 1854 while their cousin Lieutenant, later Lieutenant Colonel **Walter James Hore-Ruthven** (1838–1921), Rifle Brigade, was present at the siege of Sevastopol, and succeeded his grandmother as 9th Baron Ruthven of Freeland in 1864 and later became 1st Baron of Ruthven of Gowrie. In World War 1 he served as a Queen's Messenger and besides the Crimea medal he qualified for the British War and Victory medals, 'a unique combination'. Wilhelmina's personal estate was £5,390 and Mary Elizabeth's in the UK was £15,820. [Left. HMS *London* in Zanzibar, c.1876. Credit: © State Library of Australia and Right. Lieutenant Walter James Hore-Ruthven, RB. Photograph credit: Derek Haighton].

Augustus Thomas Hotham (1817–96)
Grave: B7/20–21 consecrated

The son of the Revd Frederick Hotham (1774–1854) and Anne Elizabeth née Hodges (1778–1862), he married Anne Bayham Stapleton (1823–71) in 1858. She died in Malta and was buried in the Ta'Braxia cemetery, Pietà where her tombstone can be seen, while he died at 17 Calverley Park without issue on 24 December 1896. Two sons of his cousin George Frederick Hotham (1799–1856) and Susan Maria née O'Brien (1804–57) took part in the war; **Charles** (c.1834–72) and **John** (1838–1807), in the army and Royal Navy respectively, and later they became the 4th and 5th Barons Hotham, though both died without issue (See Appendix 2: Woodbury Park Cemetery).

Francis George Molyneux (1805–86) and his wife
Grave A14/153–5 consecrated

The Hon. Francis George Molyneux, the fourth son of the 2nd Earl of Sefton, moved to Tunbridge Wells in 1853 and lived at **Earl's Court** – since modified and now **Molyneux Place, Molyneux Park**

Road. He died there after a long illness on 24 May 1886.[38] Two of his nephews served in the Crimea. Lieutenant **William Philip Molyneux** (1835–97), Grenadier Guards, who succeeded his father as the 4th Earl during the war, and Captain **Charles Berkeley Molyneux** (1816–92), 4th Light Dragoons, although he did not take part in the charge of the Light Cavalry Brigade. Molyneux's wife, Lady Georgina Jemima, formerly Mitford, the daughter of the 3rd Earl of Ashburnham, died in 1882 aged 77, and they are both commemorated by the 'Molyneux drinking fountain' on **Bishop's Down Road** erected by their daughter Constance Phillipina Georgina who married William Melville in 1890 and died in 1919. The personal estates of Molyneux and his wife were £49,241 and £9,452 respectively. Incidentally, Mrs Molyneux's elder brother, the Hon Percy Ashburnham (1799–1881), lived at Shernfold, Frant, and is commemorated in the parish church. [Left. Molyneux Place. Credit: Philip Whitbourn and Right: Memorial drinking fountain. Photograph by author].

Laura Mure née Markham (1804-76)
Grave A3/296 general

Laura Mure, the widow of Colonel William Mure (d.1860), DCL, MP, of Caldwell, now in East Renfrewshire, and second daughter of William Markham of Becca Hall, Yorkshire, was living at **3 Grove Hill Road** in 1861 with her unmarried daughters Anne Clementine and Laura

Elizabeth. She and Laura Elizabeth had moved to **4 Richmond Terrace (39 London Road)**, by 1871 and she died there on 10 March 1876. Mrs Mure's sons, **William** (1830–80) and **Charles Reginald** (1833–64) served in the Crimea with the 79th (Cameron Highlanders) Regiment, and later Scots Fusilier Guards, and 43rd (Monmouthshire) Regiment respectively. The younger brother participated in the 2nd Maori War and was killed in action on 29 April 1864. William married Constance Elizabeth Wyndham, a daughter of the 1st Baron Leconfield, and her sister, Caroline Sophia, was the first wife of Lieutenant Colonel **Robert Nigel FitzHardinge Kingscote**, Scots Fusilier Guards, who was one of **Lord Raglan's** ADCs. One of Mrs Mure's executors was her son William, who was MP for Renfrewshire, and nephews Clements Robert Markham and William Wickham and the solicitors they employed were Stone and Simpson, **23 Church Road**.[39] Her effects were <£3,000.

Anne Clementine Mure married Alexander Craven Ord in October 1861 and her brother-in-law, **John Redmond Ord** (c.1820–59), was with the Royal Engineers in the Crimea. At the time of the 1881 census her unmarried sister Laura Elizabeth was visiting Emma Brownville Strange, the widow of Major **John Charles Strange**, Royal Artillery, a Crimean war veteran, at 22 Cleveland Gardens, Paddington. She died shortly afterwards on 14 October 1881 at the Ord's home, Kenilworth, Hampton Road, Bristol. [Left. Richmond Terrace. Photograph by author and Right. Captain Charles Reginald Mure, 43rd Regiment, April 1864. Credit: Public Domain: New Plymouth Museum, NZ. Accession No. PHO00201400083].

William Bradley Roberts (1879–1959)
Cremated

Lieutenant Colonel Robert Bradley Roberts, DSO, Indian Army, was the fifth army son of Lieutenant, later Colonel, **Henry Bradley Roberts**, Royal Marine Artillery, who served sometime at the siege of Sevastopol with the Naval Brigade, and Augusta née Gillman.[40] He married secondly Geraldine Blanche Sullivan (d.1981) in 1912 and had issue. Living at **4 Frant Road** but he died at Whitehall Court, Westminster, aged eighty.

His executors were his daughter Helen Monica Bradley Mackenzie and the Revd James Michael Bradley Roberts. Effects £6,875. [Lieutenant Colonel Roberts. Credit: Tim Gell via ancestry. co.uk/family tree].

Dudley Alexander Charles Scott (1853–1935) and his wife
Grave A2/7–8 consecrated

Dudley Alexander Charles Scott was the third son of the Hon. Colonel **Charles Grantham Scott** (1818–85), Scots Fusilier Guards, who served for a short time in the Crimea when he left to join the 2nd Battalion in October 1854; and then retired in the following year.[41] Scott married Rose Clara Cutting (c.1877–1956) on 7 August 1909; succeeded as the 8th and last Earl of Clonmell in 1928, and had been living at 3**7 Broadwater Down** for about three years but he took no part in social work owing to ill health and died on 16 January 1935 when the earldom became extinct.[42] The dowager countess died in 1956 and was buried in the same grave.

Elizabeth Maria Spencer (1845–1928)
Grave A4/60 consecrated

Elizabeth Maria Spencer died at **2 Richmond Terrace, London Road,** on 26 February 1928.[43] She was the daughter of Brigadier General the Hon. Sir **Augustus Almeric Spencer** (1807–93), GCB, the third son of Lord Francis Almeric Spencer, 1st Baron Churchill and Helen Maria Campbell who were married in 1836. He commanded the 44th (East Sussex) Regiment in the Crimea and led the British troops engaged in the Kinburn expedition in 1855. Miss Spencer's executors were her nephews the Revd Henry Spencer Stephenson and Captain Edward Almeric Spencer. Effects £15,332. Her maternal uncle was Major General Sir **John Campbell** (1807–1855), 2nd Bt, CB, who was killed on 18 June 1855 while commanding the 1st Brigade, 4th Division, during the unsuccessful assault of the Redan. [Left. Colonel A. A. Spencer, CB, in 1859 and Right. Major General Sir **John Campbell** and his ADC Captain G. Hume (1825–91) in April 1855. Credit: Royal Collection Trust © HM King Charles III 2024: RCIN 2111146 & 2500238].

Agnes Lucy Vernon (c.1832–81) and family members
Grave A16/28–30 consecrated

Agnes Lucy, the first wife of the Hon. William Warren John Borlase Vernon and the third daughter of Sir John Peter Boileau, 1st Bt, died on 30 September 1881; and was buried at Hawkenbury together with other members of her family. Her brother Lieutenant **Charles Augustus Penrhyn Boileau**, Rifle Brigade, was wounded on 18 June 1855 and died at Malta on 1 August where he was buried, and is commemorated by a plaque in the Garrison Church, Portsmouth. Their mother, Lady Catherine Sarah, was a daughter of Gilbert Elliot, 1st Earl of Minto and one of their cousins, Lieutenant Colonel **Edmund James Elliot**, 79th (Cameron Highlanders) Regiment, died of intermittent fever in Bulgaria on 12 August 1854 before the invasion of the Crimea, while another, Major **Gilbert Elliot**, the youngest son of the 2nd Earl Minto, served with the Rifle Brigade and died at Hastings on 25 May 1865 after a long illness, aged 39. The probate register gave Mrs Vernon's address as 34 Grosvenor Place, Middlesex. Her effects were £854. [The Chaplain's Burial Register for the Garrison of Malta, 1853–1862. The National Archives: WO 156/233. Photograph by the author].

Charlotte Matilda Elizabeth Waller (née Finch) (1836- 1897) and her husband
Grave A6/20 consecrated

Charlotte Matilda Elizabeth Waller was a granddaughter of the 6th Duke of Beaufort and a grandniece of Field Marshal **FitzRoy James Henry Somerset**, 1st Baron Raglan, who commanded the British Army of the East, as the army in the Crimea was officially known, until he died from disease on 28 June 1855. She lived at **13 Belvedere Terrace, Church Road** with her husband the Revd George Waller. They died there on 23 October 1897 and 20 February 1912 and were buried in the same grave. Waller's effects were £3,430.[44] Incidentally, a pencil sketch of Lord Raglan done in the Crimea by the eminent artist **Edward Armitage** (1817–1896) was published by coincidence in

London two days after his death.[45] Armitage died 'of apoplexy and exhaustion following pneumonia' on 24 May 1896 when staying at **Mount Edgecombe, The Common,** and was buried in Brighton. [Left. The Wallers' tombstone. Photograph by author and Right. Lord Raglan 1855 by Edward Armitage. Credit: *Illustrated London News*, 30 June 1855].

Edward Hales Wilkie (1844–1911) and his wife
Graves B15/189–190 consecrated

Edward Hales Wilkie (1844–1911) lived sometime at **Springhill, London Road**, and was buried in Hawkenbury, as was his widow, Kate Louisa, née Wall, who died in 1922. His elder brother, Lieutenant, later Major General, **Hales Wilkie** (1837–91), 97th (Earl of Ulster's) Regiment, was born in Tunbridge Wells and was a pupil at Mr Allfree's school, London Road. He was present at the siege of Sevastopol and the Indian mutiny; died while commanding the infantry brigade in Malta; and was buried in the Ta'Braxia cemetery, Valletta, where his tombstone can be seen.[46]

Guy Jefferys Hornsby Wright (1871–1941)
Grave A2/207

Lieutenant Colonel Guy Jefferys Hornsby Wright, DSO, MA, a retired school master of 9 Broadwater Down died on 4 October 1941.[47] He was the son of Surgeon, later Hon. Deputy Surgeon General, **Joseph Coleman Hornsby Wright** (1830–97), MD, Royal Artillery, who was present at the battles of the Alma, Balaklava, and Inkerman, during which he was wounded by a bayonet; the siege of Sevastopol, and other later campaigns. He retired in 1880 and died in Hampstead.

**Constance Amy Ross (1864–1932), Violet Edith Ross (*c.*1867–1930).
and Ethel Marguerite or Margaret Ross (*c.*1870–1946)
Grave: A6/133 consecrated**

Three unmarried Ross sisters, two of whom were
'mental' nurses, were buried in the same grave at
Hawkenbury and according to obituary notices
in the *Courier,* their father Major **Charles Ross**
of Ivercharron, Kincardine, served with the 42nd
(Royal Highland) Regiment[48] in the Crimean War.
This is true, though Hart's Army Lists gives his
name as Captain, later Hon Major, **Joseph Charles
Ross Grove** (1834–89). He was the son of Joseph

John Grove Ross (1807–65) and Margaret Ankerville Ross (1815–1894).
First commissioned in 1851 he was present at the battles of the Alma
and Balaklava, the siege of Sevastopol, and the Indian Mutiny.[49] He
married Emily Henrietta Hay Erskine in 1860 and their three
daughters seemingly chose to use the surname Ross.

Constance Amy Ross lived sometime at **6 Guildford Road** and **20
Frant Road**, and lastly at **5 Molyneux Park Road** where she died on
13 August 1932. The funeral service was held at St Paul's, Rusthall
with the committal at Hawkenbury The family mourners included
Ethel Marguerite (Margaret) Ross (sister) and Lady Clementine
Tottenham, Lady Eveline Maud, and Major Goldie-Tautman (cousins).[50]
Probate was granted to her surviving sister. Effects £1,681.

Violet Edith Ross lived at **Southwood Corner, 78 High Street, Rusthall**
and died of a heart attack sustained while travelling on the bus from
Tunbridge Wells on 22 August 1930. She was over six foot in height
and for many years the deputy matron as St Anne's Heath, Virginia
Water, which in 19th century parlance was termed a registered
lunatic asylum. She retired to Rusthall for the last five years of her life
and took an active part in philanthropic and social work, particularly
the Infant Welfare Centre.[51] The funeral service was at St Paul's,
Rusthall and the committal at Hawkenbury. Probate was granted to
her two sisters.[52] Effects £2,325.

Ethel Marguerite or Margaret Ross, who had been a 'very keen horse-women in her younger days' was a 'lover of art and keenly interested in drama' and 'did much to popularise pastoral plays in Tunbridge Wells'. She was a 'mental' nurse by profession. She obtained the certificate of the Medico-Psychological Association[53] when at the Holloway Sanatorium Hospital, Virginia Water, 1892–94 and became a registered 'mental' nurse in 1924 when her address was **61 London Road** as it was in 1931. She then moved to **5 Molyneux Park Road** with her sister Constance. She died there on 4 October 1946;[54] and left £7,350. The funeral was at St Paul's, Rusthall and the committal at Hawkenbury. Unlike her sisters her name in the burial register was Ethel Margaret Ross Grove.

In the early part of the 20th century Ethel was employed professionally by Mrs Rachel Beer, née Sassoon (1858–1927) the widow of newspaper proprietor Frederick Arthur Beer (c.1858–1903), and the first female National newspaper editor. Rachel suffered a breakdown following her husband's death and she was 'certified by the well-known psychiatrist Sir George Henry Savage (1842–1921), MD, FRCP,[55] and committed "to the care of the commissioners of lunacy."' Mrs Beer moved to Tunbridge Wells and took a lease on **Chancellor House, Bishop's Down** (since demolished and now flats).[56] In the 1911 census she was designated a 'jewess lunatic' with Ethel Ross living there as a 'mental' nurse in charge of two other 'mental' nurses, together with five female and one male servants. In 1921 Ethel was the acting head of the **Chancellor House** household with Mrs Beer classed as a 'mental invalid'. There were two 'mental' nurses as well as six female and two male servants. Mrs Beer, who was well known locally for 'her generous interest in charity, particularly in hospitals', died at **Chancellor House** on 29 April 1927 and was buried in grave A4/61 (General) at Hawkenbury. She was an extremely wealthy woman and left £318,283 (nearly £25 million in 2024). [Major J. C. R. Grove, 42nd Regiment. Credit: Noonan Mayfair auction archive and E. M. Ross. Credit: *Kent and Sussex Courier*, 11 October 1946].

6. A servant and friend and Constantinople resident

Alice Tuck (1861–1900)
Grave: C1/697 general

Miss Tuck was for 21 years a faithful friend and servant of the family of General Sir **Robert Biddulph** (1836-1918), Royal Artillery, GCMG (1886), KCB (1896), who was present, as a lieutenant, at the battles of Alma and Balaklava and the siege of Sevastopol. He purchased the grant for the grave, with the address being **1 Montacute Gardens.**

Henry James Hanson (1838–1936) and his wife
Grave: A6/97 consecrated

Henry James Hanson's father founded the bank of Charles Simpson Hanson in Constantinople (now Istanbul) and he and his family lived in C(now K)andilli on the Asian side of Bosphorus. Henry was born there and educated in England. As a boy of sixteen he visited the Crimea and narrowly missed being hit by a Russian shot while his mother worked, presumably as an unpaid lady volunteer, in the hospital at Scutari which 'Florence Nightingale made famous the world over'. Henry continued to work in the bank for twenty-five years after his marriage to Edith Anna, the daughter of Henry Oldham, in 1863 and then moved to farm in Canada for seven years. He retired to this country and lived in the town for the last twenty-eight years of his life; sometime in **5 Hungershall Park**, where he named the house Candilli, and then **Mount Edgecombe Cottage, The Common** where he died.[57] Henry was a church warden at St Paul's, Rusthall, where his funeral service was held, and during WWI he kept the accounts of the VAD hospital in Rusthall.[58] While living in Constantinople he took a keen interest

in the development of the Crimean Memorial Church which was designed in the Gothic style by George Edmund Street, RA. The foundation stone was laid in 1858 and the building was consecrated in 1864 by the Bishop of Gibraltar, in whose diocese it lay.[59] Hanson's wife, who was 'an accomplished musician did much to establish and train the choir'. Henry James and his wife Edith Anna were buried on 20 June 1936 and 10 October 1937 respectively. Their daughter Edith Hilda (1866–1947), the widow of Arthur Hodgkin Scaife (1855–1934), was born in Candilli, died in Hampstead, and was buried in Grave A6/97 (Consecrated).

Hanson's father died in 1874 aged seventy and was buried in the Haidar Pasha cemetery on the Asian side of the Bosphorus while the tombstone of his daughter Helen Jane (1834–64), who died after just two years marriage to George Henry Clifton, has been relocated there from a cemetery in Therapia when it closed. The cemetery was opened in 1854 for the burial of military personnel dying during the Crimean War and then used for civilian burials and casualties from both WW1 and WW2.[60] [Mr and Mrs Hanson on their 70th Wedding Anniversary. Credit: *Kent and Sussex Courier*, 7 April 1933; The Crimean Memorial Church from the Bosphorus. Photograph by author; Crimean War tombstones in the Haidar Pasha cemetery photographed by Francis Bedford on 23 May 1862. The Crimean War memorial obelisk was designed by Baron Marochetti and erected in 1858. Credit: Royal Collection Trust © HM King Charles III 2024; RCIN 2861649].

Appendix 1: Holy Trinity Churchyard, Church Road

The Holy Trinity churchyard was the principal Protestant burial ground in Tunbridge Wells following the consecration of the church designed by Decimus Burton in 1829. When it became full a larger cemetery in Woodbury Park Road was opened in 1849 (See Appendix

2).The church was declared 'pastorally redundant' in 1972 but was saved from demolition and repurposed as the 'Trinity Arts Centre'; this opened in 1982.[61]

Robert William Dallas (d.1849)

Robert Dallas, a veteran of the Walcheren expedition and the Peninsular War, died on 11 September 1849 at **1 Dorset Place, Church Road**, since demolished and replaced first by Telegraph House and then Norfolk Heights, a block of flats. He was buried in the nearby churchyard of Holy Trinity. The officiating curate was the Revd **Daniel Winham** (1819–94), MA, who later served as an assistant chaplain with the British Army in Turkey, but not in the Crimea.[62] Dallas's wife Lucy, née Davidson, died in Englefield Green on 16 September 1870 and was interred at Holy Trinity with her husband. Their son Captain, later Major, **George Frederick Dallas**, (1927–88), 46th (South Devonshire) Regiment, was a pupil at the preparatory school of Thomas Robert Allfree (1796–1868) in Romanoff House, now **Vale Towers, 58 London Road**. (See Appendix 3) He was present at the battles of the Alma, Balaklava, Inkerman, and siege of Sevastopol and the second China or Opium War, and his medals are reproduced on the front cover of this monograph.

Ruth Coast née Geering (d.1845)

Ruth Geering (1780–1845) married Major, later Lieutenant Colonel, Michael Coast (1779–1830), 31st (Huntingdonshire) Regiment,[63] who

served during the peninsular war, on 21 July 1815. Their daughter Hester Louisa was born in 1820. Coast died in Ripple, Kent in 1830 while she died on 31 July 1845 and was buried at Holy Trinity. Surprisingly perhaps, the administration of her estate which was worth <£20 was not granted to her grandson Arthur Geering Day until 14 March 1866. Their daughter, Hester Louisa (b.1820) married Paymaster, later Hon. Lieutenant Colonel, **Henry Seymour Michell**, (c.1815-85), 49th (Princess Charlotte of Wales's) Regiment in 1847. He served during the first China or Opium War and was present at the battles of the Alma and Inkerman and the siege of Sevastopol;[64] retired in 1867; and died at 24 Queen Street, London on 28 January 1885 and where he was lodger in 1881.[65] Mrs Michell died on 18 June 1895 in Ventnor, Isle of Wight. Their personal estates were £9,875 and £5,136 respectively. They had no children. [Other ranks Shako badge. Author's collection].

Appendix 2: Woodbury Park Cemetery

Woodbury Park Cemetery, Woodbury Park Road, is a beautiful and important Grade II listed survival of a Victorian mortuary garden. The burial ground of Holy Trinity Church was consecrated in 1849 and remained in use until closed for new burials in the 1870s. It is now protected by its Historic Garden status and the grounds and several tombstones have been restored by the Friends of Woodbury Park Cemetery. This initiative has been rewarded by Green Flag and other awards over the years. Several of the many interesting people buried there have a connection with the Crimean War, and include:

Anna Maria Coombs, née Smoult (d.1877)

Anna Maria Coombs was living at **Fair View, Frant Road** when she died on 20 February 1877. Probate was granted to her daughter Maria, the wife of Octavius John Williamson; her effects were <£400. She was buried in the same grave as her mother Charlotte, the widow of William Smoult, who had died on 25 September 1856 aged 92. She was the widow of Lieutenant Colonel John Monckton Coombs, 10th Madras Light Infantry, who  had been murdered during 1833 by Havalidar Emam Ally while under the influence of drugs (opium) and who had mistaken him for Major Winbolt.[66] Her son, Captain **Nowell Monckton Coombs** (*c.*1822–72) served in the Crimea while on half pay from 35th Bengal Light Infantry. Shortly after he arrived he wrote two notes to Lieutenant Colonel **John Thornton Grant**, 49th (Princess Charlotte of Wales's) Regiment. These were considered 'unusual [and] exceedingly improper;' and this culminated in **Lord Raglan** demanding that Coombs make a written apology.[67] He resigned on 30 March 1855; a mere three weeks after his arrival! He died in Hastings in 1872 and probate was granted to his sister Maria Williamson of **Fairview, Tunbridge Wells**. Effects £536. [45th Bengal Light Infantry Officer's shoulder belt plate 1843–1855: Credit: www.britishempire.co.uk/forces/armyunits/indianinfantry/35thbengalinfbadge1843.htm] .

Anna Maria Eman, née Bowes (d.1883)

Mrs Eman was the daughter of General Frederick Bowes, of the EIC's service and widow of Lieutenant Colonel **James Eman**, 41st (Welch) Regiment, who was mortally wounded during the assault on Sevastopol on 8 September 1855. Two days after the

engagement, Captain, later Major General, **William Allan** – who later lived in retirement in Bidborough – wrote in a letter home: 'To-morrow the funeral takes place of our much-lamented and never-to-be-replaced Colonel; he was shot through the chest. He died this morning very peacefully; he will be a dreadful loss to our regiment. I am so sorry for poor Mrs Eman and the children, it will be a great blow to them; they are in Malta. It was only a few days ago, the Colonel read me part of a letter from her, containing a dialogue of the children about their hopes of seeing their father home safe in winter.'[68] Mrs Eman and her family came to Tunbridge Wells in November 1856 living first in **2 Belvedere, Church Road**, and then at **Saraville, at the Rusthall Common end of Nevill Park**. She then moved away and died of phthisis (tuberculosis) on 1 June 1883 at 47 West Hill, St Leonards, and formerly of 25 Stafford Street, Edinburgh, aged 54. Her effects were £871.

Her sister Ellen Selia Scott (1831–1914) was the widow of Honorary Major General Henry Young Darracott Scott (1822–93), Royal Engineers, CB (1871), FRS (1875). Formerly of Little Grange, Lamberhurst, she lived her final years at **Devonshire Cottage, St John's Road** and died on 16 May 1914 and was buried at Hawkenbury (Grave A13/127).[69] [Left. Tombstone of Mrs A.M. Eman. Photograph by author and Right. Lieutenant Colonel J. Eman: Credit: National Army Museum].

Canon Edward Hoare (1812–94)

Hoare was the influential vicar of Holy Trinity. His wife, Maria Eliza (1820–63) was the daughter of Benjamin Collins Brodie, 1st Bt, MD, FRS, and her brother, the Revd William Brodie married Lady Maria Waldegrave who was the sister of Captain **William Frederick Waldegrave** (1816–54), Viscount Chewton, Scots Fusilier Guards, who died of wounds sustained during the battle of the Alma and was buried in the Haidar Pasha cemetery, Constantinople. Her other sister, Lady Margaret Waldegrave lived sometime in **9 Park Road, Southborough**.

Lawrence Fyler (1809–73)

Samuel Fyler (d.1825) and Margaret Arnott (d.1854)[70] were married by the Revd R. Warner at the Queen Square Chapel, Bath.[71] One of their sons Lieutenant Colonel, later Major General, **Lawrence Fyler** (1809–73), was born in Twickenham and served in the Crimea with the 12th Lancers and later commanded the cavalry at

Scutari. Appointed a CB and promoted to major general in 1859 and 1868 respectively, he lived in retirement at **1 St James Road** where he died on 21 September 1873.[72] Probate was granted to his sister and residual legatee Amelia Lilias Jane (dsp.1889), wife of Richard Donoughmore Lovatt (d.1880) of Richmond Villa, Painswick, Cheltenham. His household furniture and effects and military accoutrements were auctioned by Jull and Co., Tunbridge Wells, on 22 April 1874. The militaria included a schabraque, two nearly new saddles, several bridles, General's dress and their swords, a general's full uniform, a colonel's uniform of the 12th Lancers, a collection of medals and jewellery.[73] His effects were <£1,500 while his medals are now in the Fitzwilliam Museum, Cambridge. Fyler had a troubled personal life. He married Amelia Byng (1807–79) in 1836 and the next year they had a daughter, Caroline Amelia. He was serving with the 16th Lancers in India when his solicitors published a notice stating that he would not be responsible for his wife's debts as she had been adequately provided for,[74] while his daughter had mental health issues. A report of a court case concerning her maintenance after Fyler's death recorded she was deemed 'a lunatic of imbecile mind and not able to earn her own livelihood.'[75] In 1891 she was a patient at Croft House, a private asylum, in Fairford Gloucestershire, and died there on 25 February 1906. Her executors were Captain John William Fyler, retired, and her cousin Frederica Amelia (1844–1934), née Byng, wife of Bertram Fulke Hartshorn (1844–1922).

Incidentally, Fyler was related by marriage to Mate, later Admiral, **Charles Davis Lucas** (1834–1914), Royal Navy. He had the distinction of being the first winner of the Victoria Cross on 21 June 1854 while serving on HMS *Hecla* in the Baltic. Lucas lived some time in **Great Culverden House, Mount Ephraim**, which was designed by Decimus Burton. It was demolished to make way for the Kent and Sussex Hospital, which in turn has been replaced by housing and other developments. Lucas died on 7 August 1914 and was buried at St Lawrence, Mereworth. Fylers's wife was a granddaughter of John Byng, 5th Viscount Torrington while Lucas's wife Frances Russell Hall, was a great granddaughter. [Fyler's tombstone before and after restoration. Photographs by author, and Great Culverden from the Park in the sale catalogue for the estate, 3 July 1925: Credit: Tunbridge Wells Borough Archive].

Ann Elizabeth Graydon née Rolleston (1823–74)

Mrs Graydon was the wife of Captain, later honorary Major General, **George Graydon** (1817–98), Royal Artillery, who was present at the siege of Sevastopol and the expedition to Kerch. She was the daughter of Captain James Rolleston (d.1875), Royal Navy, and his wife Ann Green, née Price, and died at their home **Monson House – now Citizens Advice Bureau – 1 Monson Way** on 4 March 1874, and was buried in the Rolleston family grave. Probate was granted to Colonel William Graydon, Bengal Army retired. Effects <£5,000.

Jenkin Homfray Llewelyn (1821–67)

Surgeon **Jenkin Homfray Llewelyn**, LSA, MRCS trained at the Bristol Royal Infirmary; was declared bankrupt following a failed business venture in 1847; first appointed an assistant surgeon in the 44th

(East Essex) Regiment in 1848.[76] Served in the Crimea with the 7th Dragoon Guards and as a staff surgeon; and in India during the mutiny with the 8th Hussars. He and his wife arrived in Tunbridge Wells in March 1867 and took up lodgings in **Stellenberg, London Road – now Regency House**. He died of heart disease on 15

May in the presence of his brother J.G. Llewelyn who was living close by at **4 Cyril Place, York Road**. Probate was granted to his widow Marian Sophia. Effects <£300. [*Cartes-de-Viste*s of Jenkin Homfray Llewelyn].

Sarah Nash née Fenton (d.1865) and her daughter

Mrs Nash was the second wife of John Nash (1807–80) whom she married in Hastings in 1861. Nash was sometime a bookseller, stationer, librarian, and postmaster in the Parade (now Pantiles) although he had seemingly retired to Hastings before the marriage. His wife

was the daughter of John Fenton of Crimble Hall in Lancashire. She died on 25 May 1865, aged 45, while her infant daughter, Josephine Mary Fenton Nash died some months later on 23 January 1866 aged 3 years 6 months. Her brother, Roger Fenton (1819–69) went to the Crimea from March to June 1855 as a civilian photographer. Images he took in the Crimea are now much admired and many are preserved in the Royal Collection and elsewhere. [Roger Fenton, self portraits, c.1854 and 1855].

Mary Philadelphia Skipwith, née Adams (d.1895), and her husband

Mary Philadephia and Fulwar Skipwith, a retired judge in the Bengal Civil Service, lived at **Avon House, 2 Garden Road**. They died on 23 June 1895 and 22 June 1883 respectively and were interred in the same grave. Skipwith's personal estate was £9,807 while hers was £12,688 and her executors were her son Colonel Gray Townsend Skipwith (d.1900), Royal Engineers; daughter Frances Annabella Skipwith (d.1915, and was buried in Woodbury Park cemetery), and nephew Francis Cadwallader Adams, (1844–1916), solicitor. Mrs Skipwith was the daughter of the Revd Thomas Coker Adams and her cousin and brother-in-law, Major General **Henry William Adams** (1805–54), 49th (Princess Charlotte of Wales's) Regiment, commanded the 2nd Brigade of the 2nd Division at the battle of Inkerman when he was severely wounded. He was evacuated to Scutari and died on 19 December 1854, with his wife Katherine at his bedside. His body was repatriated to England for burial at Ansty, and his widow was 'granted the same rank as if he had survived to the honour of KCB.' Three of his brothers served in war, namely, Commander, later Captain, **George Curtis Adams** (1807–83), Royal Navy; Lieutenant Colonel, later Major General, **Frank Adams** (1809–69), 28th (North Gloucestershire) Regiment; and Captain, later Lieutenant General and Colonel of his regiment, **Cadwallader Adams** (1825–92), 49th Regiment. [Left. Avon House, Garden Road and Right. General H. W. Adams from a family portrait. *Illustrated London News*, 10 May 1855].

John Tylden (1798–1866)

Colonel, later Major General, **John Tylden**, Royal Artillery, was the son of Osborn Tylden (1758–1827) and Anna Lloyd, née Withers. He was the Fire Master at Royal Artillery Barracks, Woolwich, at the beginning of the war and retired on full pay before the end. In 1861 he and his wife Lucy and three unmarried daughters were living at **Prospect Lodge, London Road**, just beyond Richmond Terrace; and he died in Tunbridge Wells on 29 November 1866. Probate was granted to his son Charles Ryland Tylden (1842–1915), 70th (The Surrey) Regiment, also of Tunbridge Wells. Effects <£1,000. His cousin Brigadier **William Burton Tylden** and his younger son Colonel **Richard Tylden** (1819–55) both died during the Crimean campaign. (See Section 5: Baldwin)

John Bramston Wilmot (1806–75)

Dr Wilmot, MB, MD, FRCP, was sometime the consulting physician at Tunbridge Wells Infirmary and the author of a pamphlet on the treatment of dysentery with creosote. He brought this to the attention of Dr, later Sir, **Andrew Smith** (1797–1872), KCB (Civil), MD, FRS, the Director General of the Army and Ordnance Medical Department. Smith forwarded seventy copies to Dr, later Sir, **John Hall** (1795–1865), KCB (Military), MD, the Principal Medical Officer in the Crimea, although no record of Hall's assessment of creosote's therapeutic value, or otherwise, has been found. Wilmot died unmarried on 30 April 1878 at **2 Dorset Place, Church Road** – since demolished and replaced first by Telegraph House and then Norfolk Heights. Personal estate <£7,000.

Henry Hotham (1814–1900) and his wife

The Revd Henry Hotham was a grandson of Beaumont, 2nd Baron Hotham, and in 1845 married Mary (Minnie) Hale (1810–87), the daughter of the Hon. John Hale.[77] Two sons of Hotham's cousin, Rear Admiral George Frederick Hotham (1799–1856) and Lady Susan Maria (1804–57),[78] eldest daughter of William O'Brien, 2nd Marquess of Thomond participated in the war. **Charles Hotham** (c.1834–72), 18th Regiment, was at Sandhurst in 1851 and succeeded as the 4th Baron in 1870 and died unmarried in Brighton on 29 May 1872. He was followed by his next brother, **John Hotham** (1838–1907), who also died unmarried; was a pupil at Mr Thomas Allfree's school, London Road in 1851 and then served with the Royal Navy in the Baltic, and prior to that in the West African Squadron, that was established in 1808 to help suppress the Atlantic slave trade, which had been commanded by his kinsman, a cousin of his father's, Commodore Charles Hotham (1806–55), Royal Navy, from 1846–49, and who was at the time of his death Governor of Victoria. Incidentally, on 24 June 1865 Hotham officiated at the marriage in Tunbridge Wells of his wife's niece Maria Louisa (d.1920), the daughter of the late Captain William Amherst Hale (1809–1844), 52nd (Oxfordshire) Regiment, to Major **Robert Bethune** (1827–1904), late 92nd (Gordon Highlanders) Regiment, who served in the Crimea after the fall of Sevastopol and the Indian Mutiny.[79, 80]

Appendix 3: St Paul's, Rusthall

Thomas Robert Allfree (1796–1868)

Thomas Robert Allfree went to Russia as a young man and was sometime the English tutor to the sons of Czar Nicholas I who died during the course of the war on 2 March 1855 and was succeeded by his son as Alexander II (1818–1881). In 1832 he opened a classical school [for] 'young gentlemen' in a former lodging house which he named **Romanoff House, now Vale Towers, 58 London Road**, presumably in deference to his former employer, and from whom he received a pension.[81] Pupils who took part in the war and to whom reference has been made include: Captain **George Frederick Dallas**, 46th (South Devonshire) Regiment (Appendix 1); Lieutenant, later Maj. Gen., **Hales Wilkie** (1837–91), 97th (Earl of Ulster's) Regiment (Section 5); and **John**

Hotham (1838–1907), Royal Navy, and **Charles Hotham** (1836–72), 18th (Royal Irish) Regiment (Appendix 2). Allfree died on 30 March, 1868 was buried at Rusthall as were other members of his family, and is commemorated by a stained glass window in the church. [Photograph of Vale Towers in 1934 by D.J. Johnson. Credit: The Amelia Scott, Tunbridge Wells].

Thomas Jennings Bramly (1796–1874)

Thomas Bramly and his wife Louise (1808–73) are buried at Rusthall and their son, **Alfred Jennings Bramly**, 42nd (Royal Highland) Regiment, who was present at the siege of Sevastopol and killed in action in India on 15 April 1858, is commemorated on their tombstone, together with other members of the family.

Augustus Young Earle (1829-58)

Four members of the Earle family took part in the Crimean War. Major **Augustus Young Earle** (1829–58), Royal Horse Artillery, was buried at St Paul's, Rusthall and is commemorated with a stained glass window in the church. He died on 15 September 1858 at Chalons-sur-Saône while returning home from India 'exhausted by the hardships of a soldier's life'. He was the second son of Charles Earle (1798–1881) and Emily, née Maxwell. She died in London on 9 October 1868 and was buried at Rusthall, next to her son. Of their other sons: Major **Arthur Maxwell Earle** (1833–63), 57th (West Middlesex) Regiment, died in Corfu in 1863, aged 29; and **Ralph Anstruther Earle** (1835–79), was an unpaid attaché at the British Embassy in Paris, during the years of the Crimean War. A cousin of the Earle brothers, Captain, later Major General, **William**

Earle, (1833–85), the son of Sir Hardman Earle, 1st Bt, served with the 49th (Prince Charlotte of Wales's) Regiment and was killed in the Sudan by a shot in the head. [Earle memorial window in St Paul's, Rusthall. Photograph by the author].

Frederick William Haines (c.1850–1922)

The Revd Frederick William Haines, MA, late of **Hazeldene, Pembury**, died after a short illness at Tunbridge Wells, on 25 October 1922 and was buried at Rusthall three days later.[82] He had been the vicar of Holy Trinity, Bromley Common, Kent, 1882–1903,[83] and was the son of Captain **Edward Eldridge Haines** (1815–78), 92nd (Gordon Highlanders) Regiment, who served in the Crimea during the later part of the siege.

Francis Henry Kilvington (1817–55)

Captain **Francis Henry Kilvington**, 62nd (Wiltshire) Regiment died of disease en route home from the Crimea, and was buried in Malta. His tombstone in the Msida Bastion Cemetery was destroyed by enemy bombs during World War 2 although fragments survive.[84] His widow, Elizabeth Jemima, née Inglis, installed a stained glass window in the church and when she died in 1890 a commemorative brass plaque was fixed under the window.

Thomas Abel Birmage Spratt (1811–88)

Captain, later Vice Admiral, **Thomas Abel Birmage Spratt**, CB, FRS, Royal Navy commanded HMS *Spitfire* in the Black Sea during which time he did much invaluable work as the fleet surveyor. He died at **Clare Lodge, Nevill Park** on 12 March 1888. He is commemorated by a mural plaque in the church. The funeral service was arranged by J. Booty, The Pantiles, and he was interred at Teignmouth, Devon.[85]

Appendix 4: Southborough

Albert Mitchell (c.1830–1897)

Private, later Sergeant, **Albert Mitchell** was born in Tonbridge, published his experiences with the 13th Light Dragoons in the Crimean campaign and this includes a detailed account of the charge of the Light Cavalry Brigade, during which his horse was killed.[86] He joined the Kent County Constabulary when he left the army as a sergeant in 1862. He retired in 1882 after developing kidney disease and lived at **20 Norton Road, Southborough** to which a green plaque has been affixed; and then at his sister's home at **2 Taylor Street**. He died of Bright's disease (chronic nephritis) on 16 January 1897 aged 67. His funeral was well attended and he was buried, reportedly in his uniform, at St Peter's.[87] The tombstone, which also commemorates his son, Albert Edward, who died on 7 July 1899 aged 27, was 'erected by members of the above corps as a tribute of respect to a brave and deserving comrade'. The obituary notice recorded that one of his sons was a farrier sergeant in Mitchell's own regiment. [Photograph by the author].

Daniel Price Lewis (1831–1916)
Grave reference: 3/262

Gunner **Daniel Price Lewis**, Royal Navy, was born in Dover, joined the navy in 1847 and served as a gunner in the Baltic fleet in 1854 and at the siege of Sevastopol in 1855 and was thus entitled to the Baltic and Crimea medal with clasp for Sevastopol. He married secondly Susan Elizabeth Frampton (c.1848–1903) in 1896 and was living with his third wife Mary Ann, a retired manageress of a blind institution, in **30 Vale Road, Southborough** together with his son

William Lewis a retired builder, and daughter-in-law, Annie Elizabeth, a retired head teacher. He died on 29 October 1916 and his funeral at **Southborough Cemetery, Modest Corner, Victoria Road** was attended by members of the Tunbridge Wells Veterans Association and one of his shipmates.[88] The probate register gave his address as **63 Prospect Road, Southborough** and his executor was Washington Blackhurst, a free church minister, who was living at **69 Woodlands Road, High Brooms** in 1914. Effects £864. His wife was also buried at Southborough on 23 July 1930. Incidentally, Lewis's Greenwich Hospital Pension of £25 a year was then awarded to Mr W.J. Gale, chief gunner, Royal Navy.[89] [Sailors ashore at Baro Sound, Gulf of Finland. Credit: *Illustrated London News*, 24 June 1854].

Afterword

My father, Herbert Oastler (Hugh) Hinton (1914–98), OBE, TD, and mother Gwen Elizabeth (Wendy) née Evans (1919–2013), and her two sisters Mary Macdonald (1911–2001) and Joan Evans (1916-2011) were all cremated at Hawkenbury. My father was the great grandson of Captain, later Major, **James William Dewar** (1827–60), 49th (Princes Charlotte of Wales's) Regiment, and later 97th (Earl of Ulster's) Regiment.[90, 92] He was present at the battles of the Alma and Inkerman and the siege of Sevastopol, and was appointed one of the Town Majors after the Russians had evacuated the southern part of the town. He was a widower when he went to the East as his wife, Kate Jane, née Daryell, from whom I am descended, had died in May 1853 as a consequence of a complication of her second pregnancy.

I moved to Tunbridge Wells in 1996 and found out by chance that Dewar had visited the town twice. First for few days in October 1856, together with Ensign **Randal Percy Otway Plunkett** (1832–83), 13th Baron Louth, 79th (Cameron Highlanders) Regiment, and the Misses West; and secondly in May 1857. In both cases he stayed at **Cambridge House, Cambridge Gardens**,[91, 93] the residence of Sir George and Lady Pocock who were the parents of Major **George Francis Coventry Pocock** (1830–1915), 30th (Cambridgeshire) Regiment who had been severely wounded in the Crimea with the loss of his left arm.

Following promotion to Major in 1858 Dewar transferred to the 97th Regiment which had been commanded in the Crimea by Lieutenant Colonel **Thomas Onslow Winnington Ingram** (1816–58) whose wife, Jessie Maria, née Parsons (1827–1891), was one of Dewar's cousins.[92, 94] He joined the regiment in India and married Anna Maria Charlotte de Steiger (b.c.1833) in Benares (now Varanasi) in November 1860. However, his 'constitution yielded to the unhealthy climate' and he returned to England and died a few weeks later at Middleton Stoney, Oxfordshire in the house of his younger brother Captain

William Weymss Methven Dewar (1829–1903) who spent some time in Corfu with the Oxford Militia which had been embodied during the course of the war. Dewar was buried at All Saints, Middleton Stoney, where his tombstone can still be seen. He was only 33 when he died and had been married for eight months.[93, 95]

The second Mrs Dewar provided a further association with the locality when she married Francis Alexander Randal Cramer-Roberts, who was a curate at Frant, in 1867.[94, 96] His brother John C Cramer-Roberts was the land agent for the Marquis of Camden and lived at Highfield, Bells Yew Green. A cousin of theirs, Lieutenant, later Colonel, **Charles John Cramer-Roberts** (1834–95), served in the Crimea in the same regiment as Dewar, the 49th, and this may provide an explanation of how the couple met. Anna died in 1880 while her husband was Bishop of Nassau in the Bahamas. In 1882 he married secondly Isabel Marion, the daughter of the Revd George Faithfull, who was sometime the vicar of Horsmonden. It is a small world to be sure!

Victorian terminology

This monograph has been based in large part on historical documents and some of the terms then in use are now generally regarded as either questionable or unacceptable. A particular contentious example is the Indian Mutiny and reference to it should in no way be taken as an endorsement of, or support for imperialism. In the present century there is a continuing debate about whether it is an appropriate description of the conflict or not. For further commentary on this topic see See Raugh, H.E., *The Indian Mutiny 1857–1859. A Selective Bibliography*, (Warwick: Helion, 1916) and Raugh, H.E., 'The Battle of the Books. An Indian Mutiny Historiography', *Journal of the Society of Army Historical Research*, 380 (2016), 294–313.

Acknowledgements

Over the years I have received help and advice from many people and I am grateful to them all. Sue White, Lynne Monckton, and Ann Bates have been extremely helpful in locating the graves and clarifying matters of fact etc. while other local residents who have assisted me include: Jill Armitage, Ian Beavis, June Bridgeman, Sue Brown, the late Geoffrey Copus, John Cunningham, Jan Holly, Chris Jones, Sarah Tanner, and Philip Whitbourn; and members of the Crimean War Research Society: Douglas Austin, Larry Crider, Glenn Fisher, Tony Margrave, Mike Hargreave Mawson, the late Tom Muir, and Colin Robins; and finally Colin Webb for so skilfully formatting the text for printing.

Notes and references

In addition to ones quoted below information has been obtained from national and local newspapers, the censuses from 1841, probate records, local directories, the *Annual Register Chronicle* and *Gentleman's Magazine*, and documents preserved in the British Library, London Guildhall Library, National Archives, National Army Museum, Society of Genealogists, Tunbridge Wells Library, Tunbridge Wells Borough Archive, and other libraries, and the internet including Wikipedia, ancestry.co.uk., findmypast.co.uk., and deceasedonline.com

The author and publishers have made every effort to establish the copyright of the illustrations used, including those that can be found on websites, but with no attribution, and apologise for any oversight or omissions.

1   See Mellors, C. and White, S., *'Our Beautiful Necropolis' The 150th Anniversary of Tunbridge Wells Cemetery 1873-2023,* (Friends of Tunbridge Wells Cemetery, 2023). ISBN 978-1-7394414-0-1.

2   Bates, A., Blackwell, P., and O'Meara, N., *Remembered. The Men of the First World War who Rest in the Tunbridge Wells Borough Cemetery,* (Friends of Tunbridge Wells Cemetery, 2018).

3   Baldock, P., Bates, A., Blackwell, P., and O'Meara, N., *Remembered Two. The Men and Women of the Second World War who Rest in the Tunbridge Wells Borough Cemetery,* (Friends of Tunbridge Wells Cemetery, 2019).

4   For a readable account see Small, H., *The Crimean War: Europe's Conflict with Russia,* (Stroud: The History Press, 2018).

5   Hinton, M., 'Philanthropy in Tunbridge Wells during the Crimean War', *Royal Tunbridge Wells Civic Society Newsletter,* Spring (2022), 20–21.

6   Hinton, M., 'Tunbridge Wells Peace Parade 1856', *Royal Tunbridge Wells Civic Society Newsletter*, Autumn (2020), 18–21.

7   Hinton, M., 'Some echoes of the Crimean War in Tunbridge Wells, Kent, and adjacent parishes', *Genealogists' Magazine*, 33 (2021): 9, 317–27.

8   The letters sent home by **Dallas** have been published: Mawson, M.H., *Eyewitness in the Crime'*, (London: Geenhill Books, 2001).

9   *Kent and Sussex Courier*, 1 August 1930. The museum accession number is 1930.09.

10   A similar quilt is featured in a well-known oil painting in the Hunterian Museum, Royal College of Surgeons of England by Thomas William Wood (active 1855–1872) of Private Thomas Walker, 95th Regiment, at work sewing in his sickbed.

11   **Lord Lucan's** daughter Lavinia Bingham (d.1864) married the eldest son of Field Marshal **Henry Hardinge**, **Viscount Hardinge of Lahore and Kings Newton** (1785–1856), who was Commander-in-Chief of the British Army during the war; and who lived at South Park, Penshurst. She is commemorated by the lychgate at St Peter's, Fordcombe. which was built at Lord Hardinge's expense, and a mural plaque in St John the Baptist, Penshurst. Lord Hardinge's second son, Major, later General, **Arthur Edward Hardinge** (1828–92) served in the Coldstream Guards, and was present at the battles of the Alma, Balaklava, Inkerman, and siege of Sevastopol.

12   Obituary and details of the funeral: *Sevenoaks Chronicle and Tunbridge Wells Advertiser*, 19 April 1929. Probate was granted to his widow. Effects £5,565.

13   Obituary and details of funeral including a list of members of the family and others who attended, including a nephew of Sir **Edmund Lyons**, Admiral Sir **Algernon McLennan Lyons**, GCB (1833–1908) who also served in the Black Sea Fleet: *Kent and Sussex Courier*, 29 September & 6 October 1905.

14 Obituary and details of his bequests: *Kent and Sussex Courier*, 21 & 28 February & 4 April 1913. He left his medals and sword, and CB, to his daughters Mary Isabel and Rebecca Joan respectively. His sister Ellen Mary Edridge, who had been feeble-minded since the age of sixty-two, died in 1914 and was buried in Grave B2/176 (Consecrated).

15 Probate was granted to Colonel Allan Gilmore, retired. Effects £10,197 resworn twice at £8,842 and £8,762.

16 Tony Margrave of the Crimean War Research Society, personal communication.

17 Obituary and details of funeral: *Kent and Sussex Courier*, 25 February & 4 March 1910. His son Lieutenant Charles Trevenen Holland (b.1882), Royal Field Artillery, who was killed in action in 1915, is commemorated on the tombstone and the war memorial at St Paul's, Rusthall.

18 Bequests: *Kent and Sussex Courier*, 7 November 1890.

19 Obituary: The Times, 19 January and Details of funeral: *Kent and Sussex Courier*, 29 January 1892.

20 *Kent and Sussex Courier*, 21 October 1910.

21 Dutton, R. *Forgotten Heroes. The Charge of the Light Brigade,* (Oxton: InfoDial, 2007), 378–9.

22 For details see *Kent and Sussex Courier*, 21 August 1914

23 Funeral notice: *Kent and Sussex Courier*, 11 March and *Croydon Advertiser*, 18 March 1904.

24 For details of **Marsh's** adventurous life see Memorials Inscription Group, *A Walk Round some Interesting Memorials*, (Friends of Tunbridge Wells Cemetery, 2017), 15. In 1877 he published *A Ride through Islam – A Journey through Persia and Afghanistan to India via Meshed, Herat and Kandahar*, (London: Tinsley Brothers, 1877).

25 Obituary: *Kent and Sussex Courier*, 21 December 1917 and other newspapers.

26 Obituary and details of the funeral arranged by E. Card & Co.: *Kent and Sussex Courier*, 8 & 15 January 1815.

27 *Kent and Sussex Courier*, 7 November 1919.

28 *Kent and Sussex Courier*, 3 July 1925; 16 September 1927 & 18 January 1929, with reports of the funeral arranged by Kempster and Sons.

29 A report of an assault on (the first) Mrs Love in the bar by a drunken customer gave the address as **7 Varney Street**: *Kent and Sussex Courier*, 3 April 1874. The Alma tavern was demolished during the 1970s to make way for the Royal Victoria Place shopping mall, and Boots probably covers the area in which it was situated.

30   Obituary and report of the funeral arranged by Kempster and Sons: *Kent and Sussex Courier*, 18 January 1929.

31   Report of funeral arranged by Kempster and Sons: *Kent and Sussex Courier*, 10 July 1931

32   His address where he died was not included in the notice of his death in the *Kent and Sussex Courier*, 8 June 1877.

33   Holmrook, London Road is a semidetached house previously known as Blandford House and now Nos 74–75 and is divided into flats.

34   *Kent and Sussex Courier* 7 & 14 March and Obituary: *The Times*, 7 March 1913.

35   Anon [Saunders, G.], *Manna in the Camp: or Selections of the Letters of a Medical Officer to his Wife during the Eastern Campaign in 1854–55*, (Dublin: George Herbert, 1856).

36   For details of the Tylden family see Hinton, M., 'A double Crimean War tragedy for the Tyldens of Milstead, Kent', *Genealogists' Magazine*, 34:7 (2023), 339–346.

37   *Illustrated London News* and *Dover Telegraph and Cinque Ports General Advertiser*, 21 & 22 February 1851.

38   Comprehensive obituary and details of the funeral: *Kent and Sussex Courier*, 28 May 1886.

39   *Kent and Sussex Courier*, 14 April 1876.

40   Obituary: *The Times*, 1 June 1959.

41   The Hon. C.G. Scott is commemorated by a stained glass east window in St John the Baptist, Wappenbury, Warwickshire. Two of his nephews served in the Crimea, viz. Captain the Hon. **Roger Lloyd Mostyn** (1831–99), Scots Fusilier Guards, and Captain the Hon. **Savage Lloyd Mostyn** (1835–1914), 23rd (Royal Welch Fusiliers) Regiment.

42   Obituary: *Kent and Sussex Courier*, 18 January 1935.

43   Obituary: *Kent and Sussex Courier*, 2 March and 4 May 1928. She left £15,332 gross.

44   The contents of his house were sold by Bracketts and Sons on 6 May 1912; *Kent and Sussex Courier*, 26 April 1912.

45   *Illustrated London News*, 30 June 1855.

46   Obituary: *The Times*, 24 December 1891.

47   Wright's personal estate was £35,156 net; *Sevenoaks Chronicle and Kentish Advertiser*, 9 January 1942. The burial plot was purchased by his younger brother Lionel Bache Hornsby Wright (1874-1952), MA, a retired school master, of **9 Broadwater Down**; but whose address was **53 Frant Road** when he died in a London hospital.

48   Known as the Black Watch since 1861.

49   **Ross Grove's** medals and transcripts of the letters he sent home were sold by Noonan Mayfair on 29 June 2022, Lot 163. Hammer price £4,200.

50   Obituary and report of the funeral arranged by Dust and Co: *Kent and Sussex Courier*, 19 August 1932.

51   A modern counterpart is the independent Children's Wellness Centre in Grosvenor Road.

52   Obituary and report of the funeral: *Kent and Sussex Courier*, 29 August 1930.

53   The MPA received a royal charter in 1926, with a supplemental charter giving the association the name Royal College of Psychiatrists in 1971.

54   Obituary and report of funeral: *Kent and Sussex Courier*, 11 October 1846.

55   Savage devoted himself entirely to his private practice from 1888 and drew his clientele from wealthy or well-connected London society.

56   For a photograph of Chancellor House and more information on Mrs Beer's activities as a newspaper proprietor and philanthropist see, O'Meara, N., Mellors, C., & Auckland, C., *The Caring Professions. Nurses, VADs and Radiographers*, (Friends of the Tunbridge Wells Cemetery, 2020), 36-9.

57   *Kent and Sussex Courier*, 7 April 1933 (70th wedding anniversary) & 19 June 1936 (Obituary and report of funeral arranged by H. Pink).

58   The flag which flew over the hospital is preserved in St Paul's Rusthall. Mrs Beer (q.v.) was the patron of the hospital and an important benefactor.

59   Tyack, G., The Crimean Church, Istanbul, *Cornucopia. Turkey for Connoisseurs*, Issue 25 (2002), 76–83. The archives of the church are preserved in the London Metropolitan Archive.

60   The cemetery has been in the care of the Commonwealth (formerly Imperial) War Grave Commission since the mid-1920s.

61   See Lippard, B., *Saving Trinity,* (Royal Tunbridge Wells Civic Society and Trinity Arts, 2023). ISBN 97-1-9997462-3-0.

62   The Revd **Winham** died at **Calverley Hill, Clarence Road**. The contents were sold at auction by Brackett and Sons and he was buried at Holy Trinity, Eridge,

63   Coast, the son of William Stacey and Hester Coast, was born in 1779 at Chartham, Kent; first commissioned in 1797 in the 31st (Huntingdonshire) Regiment; married Ruth Geering (b.1780) at Carbrooke, Norfolk, on 14 July 1815; promoted brevet Lieutenant Colonel in 1825 (*Sunday's Post*, 28 May 1825); and was buried on 1 June 1830 at Ripple, Kent.

64   Michell's medals were auctioned by Spink on 10–11 April 2019, lot 374.

65   The Probate Register named Lady Frances Elizabeth Michell (1829–1922), the daughter of William Legge, 4th Earl of Derby, as an executor of Michell's will. She was his sister-in-law, being the widow of his brother Major General George Bruce Michell (1805–66), Bengal Army, retired, who died on 11 February 1866 in Nice. Incidentally, two of Lady Frances's younger brothers served in the Crimean War, viz. Captain, the Hon **George Barrington Legge** (1831–1900) Rifle Brigade, and Lieutenant, later Lieutenant Colonel, the Hon. **Edward Henry Legge** (1834–1900), Coldstream Guards.

66   *The Times*, 3 February 1834, copying a report in a Madras newspaper dated 12 Oct. 1832.

67   The correspondence is in The National Archives: WO 28/108.

68   Williams, W.A. (ed.), *Crimean Letters from the 41st (The Welch) Regiment 1854–56,* (Wrexham: Bridge Books, 2011), 123.

69   *Kent and Sussex Courier*, 17 July 1914. For further details see Memorials Inscription Group, *A Walk Round some Interesting Memorials*, (Friends of Tunbridge Wells Cemetery, 2017), 11.

70   Mrs Fyler died on 8 November 1854 and her executors were her daughters Susan Jane Fyler and Amelia Lilias Jane Lovatt.

71   *Bath Chronicle*, 25th January 1798.

72   Probate was granted to his youngest sister and residual legatee Amelia Lilias Jane Lovatt. Effects <£1,500.

73   *Kent and Sussex Courier*, 17 April 1874.

74   *Durham Chronicle*, 30 May 1845.

75   *Buckingham Advertiser*, 19 December 1874.

76   *Kentish Gazette*, 23 February 1847 and *Dover Telegraph and Cinque Ports Advertiser*, 25 March 1848.

77   For information on the Hale family and their association with Woodbury Park Cemetery see: Anon, *Celebrating Jeffery Hale. The poor man's friend*, Friends of Woodbury Park Cemetery, 2016).

78   *The Standard*, 27 March 1857. She died in Tunbridge Wells and was interred at Rusthall.

79   *Kent and Sussex Courier*, 7 November 1919.

80   *Belfast News Letter*, 28 January 1865.

81   For a history of the Allfree years and later developments of the school as Rose Hill see Balowski, J., *Rose Hill 1832-2008. The History of one of Englands Oldest Prep Schools*, (Tunbridge Wells: Rose Hill School, 2008). ISBN 978-0-9560103-0-8.

82   *The Times*, 27 October 1922.

83   The church has a fine mural plaque commemorating Captain **George Herman Foreman**, 57th (West Middlesex) Regiment, who died in camp on 30 June from wounds sustained during the assault on Sevastopol on 18 June 1855.

84   The Msida Bastion Cemetery is the sole survivor of several non-catholic cemeteries on the north side of Floriana overlooking the Marsamxett or Quarantine harbour, and, like Woodbury Park Cemetery is preserved as a 19th century mortuary garden. It is the care of Din l-Art Ħelwa, the National Trust of Malta and is open to the public.

85   *Kent and Sussex Courier*, 16 March 1888.

86   Mitchell, A., *Recollections of One of the Light Brigade*, 2nd Edition, (Tunbridge Wells: Richard Pelton, 1885).

87   *Tunbridge Wells Journal*, 21 January 1897 and Chapman, F., *Tales of Old Tunbridge Wells*, (Westerham: Froglets Publications, 1999), 24–5 and McCooey, C., *Voices of Southborough and High Brooms*, (Cheltenham: The History Press, 2000), 14–6.

88   *Kent and Sussex Courier*, 10 November 1916.

89   *The Globe*, 2 December 1916.

90   Under the Childers reforms on 1881 the 97th became the 2nd Battalion of the Queen's Own Royal West Regiment; and following further amalgamations is now part of the Princess of Wales's Royal Regiment.

91   *Tunbridge Wells Gazette*, 17 & 31 October 1856 and 1 & 8 May 1857.

92   Ingram was killed at Lucknow on 14 March 1858; *Gentleman's Magazine*, August 1858, 682 and *Annual Register Chronicle,* 1858, 461.

93   Obituaries: *Bicester Advertiser*, 3 August 1861 and the *Gentleman's Magazine*, November 1861, 218.

94   The Cramer-Roberts had two children. Herbert Alexander and Evelyn Emilie born in 1870 and 1873

Publications produced by the Friends

A Walk round some interesting memorials in Tunbridge Wells Borough Cemetery

William Brentnall 1829 – 1894 – Surveyor and Engineer. A many-sided man

Memorial Symbols. A walk in Tunbridge Wells Borough Cemetery

The Forgotten Poor. Victorian Paupers in Tunbridge Wells Borough Cemetery

Guardian Angels. A brief history of angel sculpture

The Caring Professions. Nurses, VADs and Radiographers

British Missionaries to China. The Tunbridge Wells Cemetery connection

Remembered and Remembered Two. Commemorating respectively WWI and WWII casualties buried in this Cemetery

A Treasure Trove of Trees – two walks in the Cemetery

A Hundred Years of Image Making 1850 – 1950. Some of the Victorian photographers who are buried in this Cemetery.

Tunbridge Wells Worthies chosen for Queen Victoria's Golden Jubilee by Henry Peach Robinson 1887.

'Our Beautiful Necropolis' The 150th Anniversary of Tunbridge Wells Cemetery 1873 – 2023

All these publications can be purchased via our website.
https://www.friends-tw-cemetery.org/publications

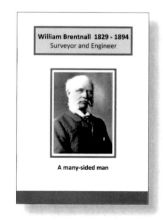

William Brentnall 1829 - 1894
Surveyor and Engineer

A many-sided man

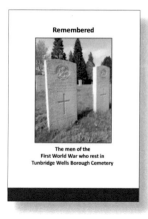

Remembered

The men of the
First World War who rest in
Tunbridge Wells Borough Cemetery

Remembered Two

The men and women of the
Second World War who rest in
Tunbridge Wells Borough Cemetery